THE NATURE KIDS GUIDE TO

CROCODILES

DAVID ANDERSON

LP Media Inc. Publishing
Text copyright © 2026 by LP Media Inc.

For information address LP Media Inc. Publishing,
30012 Variolite St NW, Princeton MN 55371
www.lpmedia.org

Publication Data

Crocodiles
The Nature Kid's Guide to Crocodiles — First edition.

Summary: "Learn all about Crocodiles, the Nature Kid Way"
— Provided by publisher.

ISBN: 979-8-89818-103-1

[1. Crocodiles – Non-Fiction] I. Title.

Title: The Nature Kid's Guide to Crocodiles

CONTENTS

SWAMPY SHORES

Snap! A crocodile rests in muddy water. Its eyes peek above the surface.

Crocodiles like to live in warm, wet places. They need water and land to survive. You can find them near rivers, lakes, and swamps. Some live in salty water near the ocean.

These reptiles love to soak in shallow water. The water keeps their bodies cool on hot days. Mud and plants hide them well.

Crocodiles also like to rest on sandy shores. They bask in the sun to warm up on rocks and logs. This way, they can move between water and dry land easily.

CROC COUNTRY

Splash! A crocodile swings it's tail. Water flies everywhere.

Crocodiles live on many continents. They are found in Africa, Asia, Australia, and the Americas.

Saltwater crocodiles live near coasts. They swim in the ocean between islands. Freshwater crocodiles stay in rivers and ponds.

Crocodiles live in many **habitats**. Some live in forests. Others live in grasslands. But they always stay close to water.

Saltwater crocodiles can swim hundreds of miles across the ocean to find new homes.

SUPER SIZED

A saltwater crocodile's head alone can be two feet long. That's the size of a car tire!

Growl! A huge crocodile crawls onto the shore. Its scaly skin glistens.

Crocodiles come in many sizes. Some are small. Others are giants.

The saltwater crocodile is the largest. Males can grow over 20 feet long and weigh more than 2,000 pounds. These big **reptiles** are longer than most cars.

Dwarf crocodiles are much smaller. They grow about 5 feet long and weigh around 40 pounds. That is less than most adult humans weigh.

TOUGH TEETH

DID YOU KNOW?
Crocodile teeth are hollow inside. This makes them lighter but they are still very strong.

Chomp! A crocodile opens its mouth wide. Sharp teeth line its jaws.

Crocodiles have between 60 and 110 teeth in their mouths. These teeth are sharp and cone-shaped, which makes them perfect for grabbing and holding **prey**.

Crocodile teeth fall out often. But new teeth grow back to replace them. A crocodile can grow up to 8,000 teeth during its whole life.

Their teeth are not made for chewing. Instead, crocodiles swallow food in big chunks. Their strong teeth grip slippery fish and other animals tightly.

SENSOR SNOUTS

A Gharial crocodile floats still in dark water. Its snout barely moves.

Crocodiles have amazing senses. Their snouts are covered with tiny bumps. These bumps can feel the smallest movements in water.

Crocodiles can sense ripples from far away. This helps them find prey even in murky water.

The gharial has an extra-long, thin snout packed with these sensors, perfect for snapping up fish with lightning-fast sideways sweeps.

Their eyes see well at night. Their ears hear sounds above and below water.

ARMORED UP

Thump! A crocodile lies on warm sand. Hard scales cover its back.

Crocodiles wear natural armor. Their backs are covered with bony plates called **osteoderms**. These plates sit under the hard outer scales.

The armor protects crocodiles from bites and scratches. It helps keep them safe from other animals.

Their belly skin is softer, though. This lets them bend and move easily. The hard back and soft belly work together to keep crocodiles both safe and flexible.

Osteoderms contain blood vessels that help crocodiles absorb heat from the sun.

MEATY
MENU

Crunch! A crocodile bites down on a catfish. Bones crack loudly.

Crocodiles eat meat. They hunt fish, birds, and mammals. They also catch crabs and frogs.

Big crocodiles eat larger animals. They can catch deer, wild pigs, and buffalo. Smaller crocodiles stick to smaller prey.

Crocodiles do not eat every day. One big meal can last them for weeks. Their bodies use food very slowly. This helps them survive when food is hard to find.

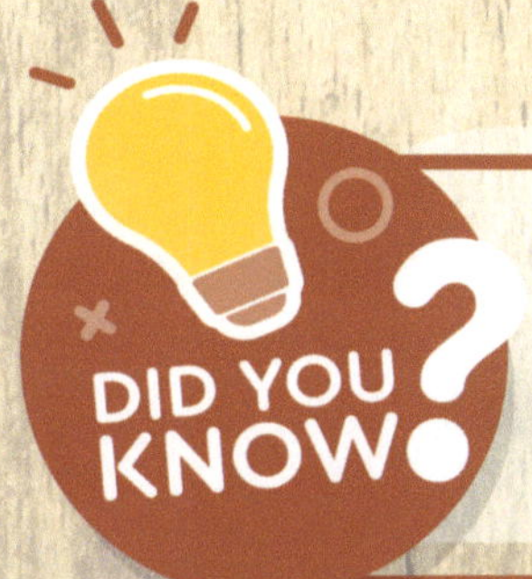

Crocodiles will swallow stones to help digest the chunks of food they swallow whole.

SNEAK
ATTACK

Swoosh! A crocodile glides toward the shore. Its body stays hidden.

Crocodiles are sneaky hunters. They wait in shallow water near the edge. Only their eyes and nostrils show above the surface.

They stay very still. They watch animals come to drink. Then they strike fast.

A crocodile lunges out of the water. It grabs prey with its strong jaws. In less than one second, it pulls the animal underwater.

Once underwater, crocodiles spin their bodies fast. This move is called a death roll.

Crocodiles have the strongest bite of any animal – over 3,700 pounds of pressure!

WATCH OUT

Screech! A bird flies away fast. A crocodile waits below.

Birds, fish, and small mammals stay alert around crocodiles. They know crocodiles might be hiding.

Some animals have warning calls. They make loud sounds when they spot a crocodile. This helps other animals escape in time.

Many animals drink quickly to stay safe. They watch the water carefully and stay ready to run at any moment.

Hippos are one animal that is too big for crocodiles to attack. Adult Hippos weigh over 3,000 pounds!

DIVE DEEP

Whoosh! A crocodile dives deep and vanishes from sight.

Crocodiles dive to stay safe. They sink below the surface when danger comes near. The deep water hides them well.

Crocodiles can hold their breath for a long time. Some stay underwater for over an hour. Their heart rate slows down to save air.

They also dive to cool off. Deeper water feels cooler on hot days.

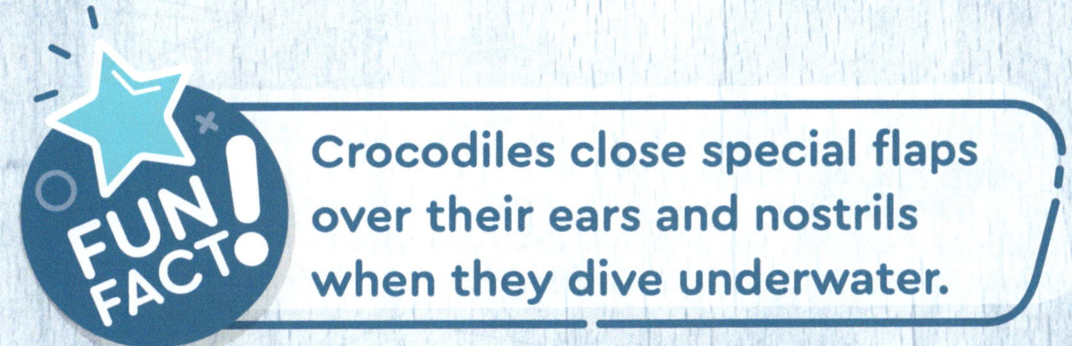

GLIDE AND GALLOP

24

Rumble! A crocodile runs across dry land. Its legs move fast beneath it.

Crocodiles move in different ways. In water, they tuck their legs close. Their strong tails push them forward.

On land, crocodiles can walk or run. They lift their bodies off the ground. Their legs carry them quickly.

Some crocodiles can gallop for short bursts. This lets them reach speeds up to 11 miles per hour!

Crocodiles have webbed back feet to help steer underwater. Their strong tails do most of the swimming work.

LAZY LOGS

One meal can last a crocodile for months. They digest food slowly and use little energy at rest.

Snarl! A crocodile lies flat on a sunny bank. Its eyes watch the water.

Crocodiles rest much of the day. They lie still on banks or float in water. Sun basking warms their bodies.

They need this heat because they cannot make their own body heat like mammals. Crocodiles are cold-blooded animals. That means their body temperature changes to match the air or water around them.

When too hot, they open their mouths wide. This helps cool them down. Some rest with jaws open for hours.

FLOAT
FRIENDS

Many crocodiles gather on a riverbank. They rest side by side.

Crocodiles sometimes live near each other. A group is called a float. Together, they share the same water and land.

Bigger crocodiles often get the best spots. Smaller ones must stay farther away.

Crocodiles do not hunt together. Each one catches its own food. They live near each other but do not work as a team.

Crocodiles use sounds and body slaps to communicate with others in their group.

BELLOWING

BACHELORS

A male crocodile lifts his head high and bellows loud.

Male crocodiles make loud sounds. They bellow to attract females. Their bellows travel far across the water.

Males also slap their jaws on the surface. This slapping makes big splashes. Females can hear and feel these signals.

Larger males often bellow more. Their calls are deeper and louder, which draws females closer.

When a male crocodile bellows, water on his back dances and sprays into the air!

CUTE HATCHLINGS
DID YOU KNOW?
A mother crocodile can lay about 20 to 80 eggs in one nest. She covers them with plants and mud.

Squeak! Tiny crocodile babies break out of their eggs.

Baby crocodiles are called **hatchlings**. They come from eggs buried in nests. Each egg is about the size of a chicken egg.

Hatchlings are very small. They measure about 12 inches long. Their teeth are tiny but sharp.

Young crocodiles can swim right away. This helps them catch bugs and small fish.

Many hatchlings stay near their mother. She guards them from danger. Even so, only a few hatchlings survive to become adults.

CARING CROCS

34

Grunt! A mother crocodile digs into her nest mound.

Mother crocodiles guard their nests. They stay close for about three months to keep eggs safe from predators.

When babies hatch, they make squeaking sounds. The mother hears them and digs them out. She is very gentle with her young.

Some mothers carry babies in their mouths to move them safely to the water. The babies ride inside without getting hurt.

Mothers protect their young for weeks or months. They chase away any animals that come too close.

TROUBLED TIMES

Crack! A crocodile crawls past broken trees. The swamp looks empty.

Crocodiles face many dangers today. People hunt them for their skin, which is used to make bags and shoes.

Habitat loss is another big problem. Wetlands are drained for farms and buildings. This leaves crocodiles with fewer places to live.

Pollution also hurts crocodiles. Dirty water makes them sick.

Crocodile farms help wild crocs! By raising crocs for leather, fewer wild ones are hunted for their skins.

HELPING
HANDS

Chirp! A crocodile swims slowly in a protected river.

People work hard to save crocodiles. Many countries now protect them with laws. Hunting crocodiles is against the law in most places.

Some groups also raise baby crocodiles safely. They keep them in special pools. Later, they release them into the wild.

These efforts help crocodile numbers grow again. Scientists count crocodiles each year to track their progress.

American crocodiles were once very rare. Now thousands live in Florida thanks to protection.

GLOSSARY

reptiles
Cold-blooded animals with scaly skin that lay eggs.

osteoderms
Hard bony plates under a crocodile's skin that protect it like armor.

prey
An animal that is hunted and eaten by another animal.

habitats
Places where animals live and find food and water.

hatchlings
Baby animals that have just come out of their eggs.